D0860340

# Rookie
### Read-About®
Science

# What's the Difference?
# Cheetahs and Leopards

### by Lisa M. Herrington

### Content Consultant
Dr. Lucy Spelman

### Reading Consultant
Jeanne M. Clidas, Ph.D.
Reading Specialist

**Children's Press®**
An Imprint of Scholastic Inc.

Library of Congress Cataloging-in-Publication Data

Herrington, Lisa M., author.
  Cheetahs and leopards / by Lisa M. Herrington.
    pages cm. -- (Rookie read-about science. What's the difference)
  Summary: "Introduces the reader to cheetahs and leopards"-- Provided by publisher.
  ISBN 978-0-531-21481-7 (library binding) -- ISBN 978-0-531-21529-6 (pbk.)
  1. Leopard--Miscellanea--Juvenile literature. 2. Cheetah--Miscellanea--Juvenile literature. 3. Children's
questions and answers. I. Title.

  QL737.C23H458 2016
  599.75--dc23
                                                    2015017325

Produced by Spooky Cheetah Press
Design by Keith Plechaty

© 2016 by Scholastic Inc.

Photographs ©: cover right: Steve Bloom Images/Shutterstock, Inc.; cover left: Winfried Wisniewski/Media
Bakery; 3 top left: Eric IsselTe/Thinkstock; 3 top right: Volodymyrkrasyuk/Dreamstime; 4 top: Volodymyr
Krasyuk/Shutterstock, Inc.; 4 bottom, 7 bottom: Eric Isselee/Shutterstock, Inc.; 7 top: Volodymyr Krasyuk/
Shutterstock, Inc.; 8 top: Martin Harvey/Getty Images; 8 bottom: Valdecasas/Shutterstock, Inc.; 11 main:
Stuart G Porter/Shutterstock, Inc.; 11 left inset: Biosphoto/Shutterstock, Inc.; 11 right inset: Callan Chesser/
Dreamstime; 12 main, 12 inset: EcoPic/iStockphoto; 15 main: Pushish Donhongsa/Shutterstock, Inc.; 15
inset: Modi1980/Dreamstime; 16: James Warwick/Getty Images; 19: Minden Pictures/Shutterstock, Inc.;
20: Suzi Eszterhas/Nature Picture Library; 23: Minden Pictures/Shutterstock, Inc.; 24 inset: age fotostock/
Shutterstock, Inc.; 25: imageBroker/Shutterstock, Inc.; 26: Birgit Koch/age fotostock; 27: Modi1980/
Dreamstime; 28 top: Andy Rouse/Nature Picture Library; 28 bottom: Terry Whittaker/FLPA/age fotostock;
29 top: Krzysztof Wiktor/Shutterstock, Inc.; 29 inset: Amazon-Images MBSI/Alamy Images; 29 bottom:
Boleslaw Kubica/Dreamstime; 30: J Reineke/Shutterstock, Inc.; 31 top: erichon/Shutterstock, Inc.; 31 center
top: Martin Harvey/Getty Images; 31 center bottom left: Biosphoto/Shutterstock, Inc.; 31 center bottom
right: Callan Chesser/Dreamstime; 31 bottom: Modi1980/Dreamstime.

Map by XNR Productions, Inc.

# Table of Contents

# Which Is Which?

They are both big cats. They both have black spots on their fur. They both hunt other animals for food. But which is a cheetah and which is a leopard?

Did you guess right? Cheetahs and leopards are a lot alike. But they are not exactly the same. There are ways to tell them apart.

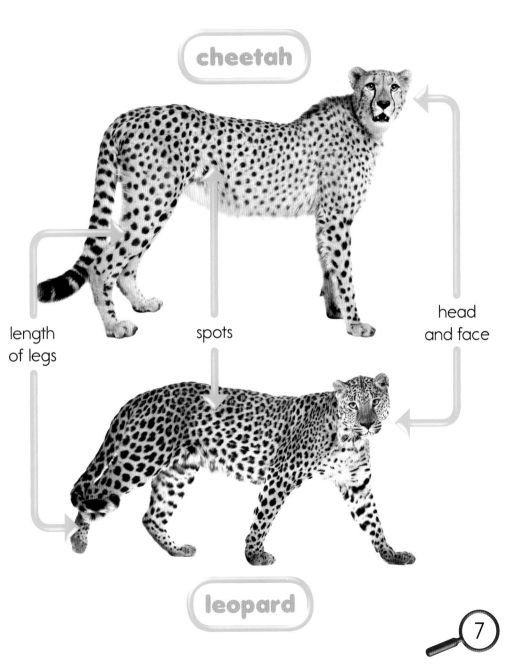

cheetah

length
of legs

spots

head
and face

leopard

7

# Big Cat Bodies

What is an easy way to tell a cheetah from a leopard? Take a look at their bodies.

A cheetah's long, thin body is built for speed. It has long legs that help make it the fastest land animal.

A cheetah's claws grip the ground so its paws do not slip as it runs. The claws never fully **retract**. The cheetah cannot pull them all the way back into its paws.

A leopard's body is built for power. Leopards have heavier bodies and shorter legs than cheetahs.

Leopards retract their claws when they run. The claws come out when the leopard is ready to climb or grab something.

Leopards are excellent climbers.

claws out

claws in

# "Spot" the Difference

Cheetahs and leopards both have tan fur with dark spots.

A cheetah's spots are black and round. It has just a few spots on its face. It also has one dark stripe under each eye. The stripes keep the sun from shining right in the cheetah's eyes.

A leopard's spots are called **rosettes** (ROH-zets). They are shaped like small roses. Some of the spots are solid black. But most have a tan center with a black outline.

A leopard has a larger head than a cheetah. It has many spots on its face.

A cheetah races after a Thomson's gazelle.

16

# On the Hunt

Cheetahs hunt during the day. They use speed to catch their **prey**. They need light to see where they are going as they race across the large, open **grasslands**.

Cheetahs often eat gazelles and rabbits. The cheetah quietly gets as close as it can to its prey. Then it chases it down with a burst of speed.

Leopards use strength to kill their prey. They hunt at night so they can stay hidden. They sneak up on an antelope, a deer, or a wild pig. Then they pounce!

They carry their meal high into a tree. It will be safe from other animals there.

This leopard carries an impala up a tree.

# Bringing Up Babies

Most cheetahs live alone. Some males live in small groups with their brothers.

Cheetahs usually have three to five cubs. They stay with their mom for about two years. Cheetah moms teach their cubs how to hunt. Cubs also play with each other and their mom. That teaches them how to hunt and keep themselves safe.

Adult leopards live alone.

Leopards usually have two to four cubs. They stay with their mother for about two years. Leopard moms teach their cubs how to hunt and stay safe.

The cubs play and chase each other. This is how they practice hunting. They are learning how to survive on their own.

Now you can "spot" the difference between these animal look-alikes!

# Cheetahs and Leopards

Most cheetahs live in Africa. A small number live in Asia. Leopards are also found in Africa and Asia.

Leopards live in more places than any other wild cat.

**North America**

**South America**

## MAP KEY

 Cheetah range

 Leopard range

24

# Around the World

Fewer than 100 cheetahs live in Asia.

Europe

Asia

Africa

Australia

Antarctica

# What's the

small head; fewer spots on face

long, thin body

solid, round spots

long legs

**cheetah**

26

# Difference?

large head; many spots on face

rosettes (spots shaped like roses)

thick, heavy body

short legs

leopard

Cheetahs are the only big cats that do not roar. Sometimes they growl or purr. Mother cheetahs make a chirping sound to call their cubs.

King cheetahs have blotches and stripes instead of spots. There are not many king cheetahs left in the world.

# Amazing!

Most cats do not like to get wet. But leopards are strong swimmers. They sometimes catch fish to eat.

Some leopards have black fur. They are called black panthers. They still have spots, though. You just have to look closely to see them!

close-up of fur

# Guess Who?

✓ My spots are black and round.
✓ My body is thin with long legs.
✓ I have a small head with dark stripes under my eyes.

**Am I a leopard or a cheetah?**

Answer: cheetah

# Glossary

**grasslands** (GRASS-lands): large open areas of grass

**prey** (PRAY): animal that is hunted by another animal for food

**retract** (REE-trakt): pull something back into another thing that covers it, as a leopard retracts its claws

**rosettes** (ROH-zets): spots on a leopard's coat that are shaped like roses

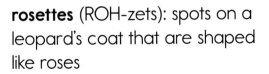

# Index

# Facts for Now

Visit this Scholastic Web site for more information
on cheetahs and leopards:
**www.factsfornow.scholastic.com**
Enter the keywords **Cheetahs and Leopards**

# About the Author

Lisa M. Herrington has written many books and articles about
animals for kids. She lives in Trumbull, Connecticut, with her husband,
Ryan, and daughter, Caroline.